SWALLOWED BY A WHALE —TWICE

Paul & Debbie —
Thanks for the support!

SWALLOWED BY A WHALE TWICE

RICK POST

Swallowed by a Whale – Twice
Published by Potential Resources, Little Canada, MN 55109

Edited by Carol King
Interior Design and Layout by Gretchen Miller
Cover Design by Justin Post
Cover Layout by Eric Beavers

Hardcover ISBN	*- 978-0-9996510-0-1*
E-book ISBN	*- 978-0-9996510-1-8*

Printed in the United States of America

DEDICATION

This book is dedicated to my wife Beth and my children, Justin, Kala and Sean, and Colin and Katelyn. Without their support, encouragement and help this book would never have made it to print. They were the ones who lived with me during my seasons of challenge and were always there to support me during some difficult times!

I would not be the person I am today or on the journey that I am on without the love and support of my wife Beth! She has been there by my side for almost 32 years of marriage. I am so blessed to have her by side in the journey of our life together! She is my rock and encourager who always helped me make it through the challenges I have faced over the years.

Thanks to my kids who helped with the design, edits and content reviews throughout the writing process! Thanks for helping me make my dream become a reality!

TABLE OF CONTENTS

FOREWORD ix
1 | THE CALLING 1
2 | THE RESPONSE 7
3 | GOD'S REACTION 15
4 | EMOTIONS OF LOSS 21
5 | THE PRAYER 25
6 | THE JOURNEY 29
7 | THE CALLING 39
8 | MY STORY 47
9 | MISSING THE POINT 55
10 | WHY SHOULD WE CARE 67
11 | OOPS IT HAPPENED AGAIN 71
BIBLIOGRAPHY 79

FOREWORD

This book has been in my head for several years, but I never took the time to get it written out. Without the encouragement of my family these words would probably still be in my head. But God made it clear to me that I needed to get the concepts in this book out of my head and onto a printed page.

Swallowed by a Whale – Twice is the story of how God has changed me and made me who I am today. I believe there are five groups of people, others like me, who will find it useful:

- People who have sensed God working in their life and that He is trying to send a message to them to do something for Him.

- People who have gone through the loss of a job and the impact that can make in their life.

- People who have gone through a season of struggle and criticism and need to find out what is on the other side of that struggle.

- People who put God in a box and just take Him out on Sunday mornings or special occasions or really don't know God on a personal level.

- People who are on an adventure to figure out who they are and how their past has influenced the person that they have become today.

Join me on a journey through the life of Jonah as we examine his experiences and interactions with God to see both their significance in my life, and what you might learn from them as well.

My hope and prayer is that as you read Swallowed by a Whale – Twice, you will be challenged to take a deeper look at who God has made you to be and what you are doing to respond to the calling of God on your life.

1 | THE CALLING

The Lord gave this message to Jonah son of Amittai: "Get up and go to the great city of Nineveh. Announce my judgement against it because I have seen how wicked its people are." Jonah 1: 1,2 NLT

I don't know about you, but I have never had as clear a message from God as Jonah did here. Today God communicates with us in a variety of ways, some not even available to Jonah at this time when he lived nearly three thousand years ago. It may be that you experienced some kind of trial or testing or challenge that you must respond to. Or, it could be as simple as understanding that the message or passage you are reading in Scripture is calling you to some specific response.

Whatever form it takes, hearing from God with a direction or specific plan was a really hard concept for me to understand when I got my first message that I recognized as from God. I was so busy in life doing things, that I did not allow time to listen and hear from God. I was doing good things for God, or so I thought, but mostly doing things for myself.

Let me set the context here. My first recollection of God directing me to something else happened in April of 2011. At the time, I was a Director of IT for Target Corporation and was coming up on celebrating my 20- year anniversary with the company. My wife, Beth, had just resigned her position as Kids Director at Eagle Brook Church, and in her search for God's direction, she began mentioning that perhaps I should quit my job and we should do ministry together.

My answer was my usual response – when I retire from work, then I will do something like that. At work, I had just received a promotion and a large salary increase that made up for the salary lost when Beth quit her job. I felt pretty confident that I was where God wanted me.

My second message from God came in August of 2011. I was attending the Leadership Summit put on by the Willow Creek Association. One of the speakers was Steven Furtick from Elevation Church. He talked about digging ditches. He said we need to take action, starting by digging ditches, laying the foundation and trusting God to provide what is needed for the rest.

At the end of the summit, Bill Hybels spoke about the need for business leaders to finish strong, and for some to leave their places of employment and go into ministry. The conference leadership team then provided each attender with a piece of a broken clay pot and asked us to write on it what God was saying to us. I remember writing **"8/12/2011 WHAT??"** I was sensing God was directing me to take action, but I did not know what it was.

Following the summit, I purchased "Sun Stand Still" by Steven Furtick, a book I became interested in when I heard him speak, and began reading it. In his book, Furtick challenges his readers to take a step of audacious faith. Audacious faith is a daring faith, a risk-taking faith. It is trusting God for something or to do something beyond what your normal capacity might be.

I read the first eights chapters, and at the end of chapter eight is a pledge of audacious faith:

> *"By God's grace, no matter what it costs me, I'm going to live by audacious faith. I'm going to believe God for the impossible, to accomplish by and for him what I cannot accomplish on my own. No matter what people think about my vision for my life, I'm going to take God at His word. I'm going to trust Him with my whole heart and follow Him step by step, even when my surrender requires sacrifice. Even if it seems like He's taken me over the edge, I will trust that He'll be there to catch me if I fall. I will trust that He is*

good and that somehow, someday, He will work all things in my life together for my good and His glory." 1

I remember praying that pledge on September 18th, 2011 and I wrote in my journal the following:

~~~

...And it is impossible to please God without faith. Anyone who wants to come to Him must believe that God exists and that He rewards those who sincerely seek Him. Hebrews 11:6 NLT

What is my faith like? Do I have faith to ask God for great things? What is my "audacious" prayer? What does God want to do with my life?

As we move into a new stage of life with our kids off to college and us as empty nesters, it is a good time to ask the question, what does God want to do with our lives? Where does He want us to get involved? What act of faith is He calling us to?

It is a time of personal change and reflection to search out His plans for our lives.

Prayer – please give me the faith to do great things for You. Help me to know what You want me to do that I can only do because of You and with Your help!

~~~

Let me just say this, be careful what you pray for, because if you mean it, God is going to take you at your word and do something with it.

---

1 (Furtick, Sun stand still: what happens when you dare to ask God for the impossible 2010, 92)

I wonder if that was what happened to Jonah. Was he praying to God and asking to be used by God? When God spoke to him was he expecting something easy? Did he expect to be asked to go Nineveh? I doubt it.

When I asked God to give me faith to do something for Him, I was expecting it was going to be something simple that would not cost me much and that I could fit it in to my already busy schedule without having to change or give up much. I wonder if I was a bit like Jonah?

REFLECTION QUESTIONS

- Have you ever sensed God was somehow communicating His will or speaking to you? How did you respond to it?

- What things are keeping you so busy in life that you do not have time to hear a message from God?

- Have you ever asked God to speak clearly to you about a direction in your life? What did you do to prepare yourself to hear God's message?

- What are you willing to let go of in order to respond to God's message to you?

2 | THE RESPONSE

Jonah lived during the reign of Jeroboam II and these events took place somewhere between 786 and 746 BC. Jeroboam II was the King of Israel after the tribes split into two kingdoms after Solomon's reign. Nineveh was the capital of Assyria, not only the enemy of Israel but also a major world power at the time. In Jonah 1:1 and 2 we see that God told Jonah to go to Nineveh and announce his judgement to them. God asking Jonah to go to Nineveh would be like God asking me to go to Moscow in Russia and announce their judgement. So how did Jonah respond?

> *"But Jonah got up and went in the opposite direction to get away from the Lord. He went down to the port of Joppa, where he found a ship leaving for Tarshish. He bought a ticket and went on board, hoping to escape from the Lord by sailing to Tarshish" Jonah 1:3 NLT*

Jonah wanted nothing to do with saving the people of Nineveh. He probably feared for his life and what they would do to him if he came in telling them of God's judgement. So, he got on a boat heading in the opposite direction to get away from Nineveh, even if God was leading him there.

How do we respond when we sense God is calling us? I think people respond to God's calling in several different ways. Obviously, the best response is to say "Yes" and do what God is asking you to do.

Saul did this on the road to Damascus. He was blinded by a bright light and heard Jesus talking to him and calling him to ministry. Saul followed God's direction and he went back to his Roman name, Paul, an apostle and author of much of the New Testament. Many people don't respond as directly and completely as Paul did for a variety of reasons such as fear, lack of faith, avoidance or distraction.

For me, the response was **"Not Now."** I had things that needed to be finished first. I had three kids in college with lots of tuition bills yet to pay. I had a good job, a great salary and I had my plan and future all figured out, or so I thought. Seven more years of work and I could retire from Target and then I would do whatever God wanted me to do. I would be in control because I would not have to worry about a salary and I could provide for my own expenses. I had "Golden Handcuffs." I made too much money to ever think I could survive on a ministry income. I was in control and that was right where I liked to be.

My guess is that for many of us, this is the response we have given to God when He has asked us to do something for Him. We will do that when we have more time or when we finish something else first. We may not get on a boat and go in the opposite direction like Jonah, but we find things to occupy our minds and time so that we don't think about what we are avoiding or running away from. Satan often fills out lives with busyness so that we do not have the time to hear God. And even if we hear Him, we think that there is no way we can do it.

However, I think the biggest reason why people don't respond to God's call is **fear**. Satan loves to fill us with fears, raising questions in our mind about whether we are good enough or capable enough to do what God is calling us to do. Moses is a great example of this. God called him to lead the Israelites out of Egypt. Five times Moses protested and said he was not qualified or good enough. God responded five times to Moses' fears and objections. God's responses to Moses should help us when we are dealing with our own fears when God asks us to do something. **Remember, our fear is really our lack of faith and that results in doubt.**

In Exodus three we see how Moses responds to God's call. God talks to Moses through the burning bush and says the following:

> *"Now go, for I am sending you to Pharaoh. You must lead my people Israel out of Egypt. But Moses protested to God, Who am I to appear before Pharaoh?* ***Who am I*** *to lead the people of Israel out of Egypt?" Exodus 3:10,11 NLT*

Moses's first fear was **Insecurity – Who am I?** Many of us feel insecure when God asks us to do something. We don't feel qualified to do what God calls us to do. However, God doesn't expect us to have our act together when He calls us. He delights in helping to get us ready or qualify us. II Corinthians 3: 5-6 says it best:

> *"It is not that we think we are qualified to do anything on our own. Our qualification comes from God. He has enabled us to be ministers of His new covenant. " II Corinthians 3:5-6 NLT*

I have to remind myself often that **God calls us so that He will be glorified**. Too often I forget this and do my work or even ministry in such a way that I get the recognition. However, God calls me as I am, many times totally unqualified, so that He will be glorified. Remember, Paul was a brilliant man and trained to be a great orator…so he was qualified as a speaker. He just started out with the wrong message. Moses is a different case. It appears he probably stuttered. See how God responds to Moses.

> *God answered, I will be with you. And this will be your sign that I am the one who has sent you: When you have brought the people out of Egypt, you will worship God at this very mountain." Exodus 3:12 NLT*

And Moses responded.

> *But Moses protested, "If I go to the people of Israel and tell them, 'The God of your ancestors has sent me to you' they will ask me, 'What is his name?' Then what should I tell them?" Exodus 3:13 NLT*

Moses's second fear was **Credibility – Who and why will anyone believe me?** What would make people accept me as someone doing the work of God? And why should they accept me? We deal with a world that doubts whether God even exists.

People may be skeptical and could be quick to question whether to accept your calling. This is something many of us feel. I feel I don't have the right education or background to do God's work. I always believed I needed to have a seminary degree so that people will know that I speak for God. I struggled with how I would ever convince people to listen to or follow me?

God's second response:

> *God replied to Moses, "I AM WHO I AM. Say this to the people of Israel: I AM has sent me to you." God also said this to Moses, "Say this to the people of Israel: Yahweh, the God of your ancestors – the God of Abraham, the God of Isaac, and the God of Jacob – has sent me to you. This is my eternal name, my name to remember for all generations." Exodus 3:14,15 NLT*

God went on in Exodus three to tell Moses that he will be accepted by the leaders of Israel and that the King of Egypt will need to be convinced. God also told Moses that He would perform miracles and the people of Israel will be allowed to leave Egypt with great gifts given to them by the people of Egypt. But that was still not enough to convince Moses to act.

Once again Moses protests a third time.

> *But Moses protested again, "What if they won't believe me or listen to me? What if they say, "The Lord never appeared to you?" Exodus 4:1 NLT*

Moses is still struggling with obedience. This time we see his third fear – **Fear of Failure** – the single most powerful fear that holds me back. My fall back has always been, "I don't want to fail, so it's better to not try at all." We all can think of things we have wanted to do, or even felt led to do, but we have said "No" because we didn't feel like we could do it well enough.

But God responds to this protest with a group of miracles that He will do through Moses – turning a staff into a snake, turning his hand into a diseased hand and then curing it and turning water into blood. However, that was still not enough for Moses. He had a fourth protest:

> *But Moses pleaded with the Lord, "O Lord, I'm not very good with words. I never have been, and I'm not even now, even though you have spoken to me. I get tongue-tied, and my words get tangled." Exodus 4:10 NLT*

Moses is still pleading with God, this time laying out his fourth fear – **Public Speaking** – a fear that I too have struggled with most of my adult life. I feel that I am not a good speaker; I get nervous in front of people. This fear has held me back on many occasions. "Have someone else say it" or "They are better than me" are the lies that I have told myself. I will share more about this fear later in the book.

I love God's response in the next verse:

> *Then the Lord asked Moses, "Who makes a person's mouth? Who decides whether people speak or do not speak, hear or do not hear, see or do not see? Is it not I, the Lord? Now go!* ***I will be with you as you speak****, and I will instruct you in what to say." Exodus 4:11,12 NLT*

Maybe you are like me. We need to remember those words and find comfort in them when we struggle with our fears. Although this promise was given to Moses, we find similar encouraging words in the New Testament. Here are two verses that I find very helpful.

> *"Teach these new disciples to obey all I have given you. And be sure of this: I am with you always, even to the end of the age." Matthew 28:20 NLT*

> *"You can ask for anything in my name, and I will do it, so that the Son can bring glory to the Father. Yes, ask me for anything in My name, and I will do it!" John 14:13-14 NLT*

But Moses objected a fifth time.

> *But Moses again pleaded, "Lord, please! Send anyone else."*
> *Exodus 4:13 NLT*

Moses still struggles with God, this time perhaps we hear what he is really feeling, the fifth and final fear – of **Responsibility** – of being the person accountable for the results and personally, I struggle with working under that pressure. "Use someone else." This is the last hesitation, but often this is really the root of all the other objections. We just don't want to do what God is asking us to do.

This gets at the inner core of our faith and willingness to let go of our comforts and what we know as normal. So often, we don't want to give up our control. This was what was holding me back. I liked my routine. I liked the income I had and the freedom that came with it. I thought I was doing enough for God as I was generous in my tithes and offerings, I attended church regularly and I served in various volunteer roles over the years.

I learned that God didn't want my things, God wanted me!

Here is how God responded to Moses's final objection:

> *Then the Lord became angry with Moses. "All right," he said. "What about your brother, Aaron the Levite? I know he speaks well. And look! He is on his way to meet you now. He will be delighted to see you. Talk to him, and put the words in his mouth. I will be with both of you as you speak, and I will instruct you both in what to do. Aaron will be your spokesman to the people. He will be your mouthpiece, and you will stand in the place of God for him, telling him what to say. And take your shepherd's staff with you, and use it to perform the miraculous signs I have shown you."*
> *Exodus 4:14-17 NLT*

Notice in the end God did not let Moses off the hook. He provided a spokesperson to help Moses overcome his fears, but he still sent him on to complete what God wanted him to do. We may think our fears will justify ignoring our calling, but, in reality we are only delaying the blessing and joy that God has for us in following His lead.

In the next chapter, we will see what it took for Jonah and me to overcome our fears and follow God's calling.

REFLECTION QUESTIONS

- What are the fears you struggle with when you are wrestling with following God's call for your life?
- What keeps you from saying "Yes" when you sense God is asking you to do something?
- How can you use God's responses to Moses to help you overcome your own fears?

3 | GOD'S REACTION

When we do our own thing, and ignore God's call or direction, God can choose to take action to get our attention. See what happened to Jonah:

> *But the Lord hurled a powerful wind over the sea, causing a violent storm that threatened to break the ship apart. Fearing for their lives, the desperate sailors shouted to their gods for help and threw the cargo overboard to lighten the ship. But all this time Jonah was sound asleep down in the hold. So the captain went down after him. "How can you sleep at a time like this?" he shouted. "Get up and pray to your god! Maybe he will pay attention to us and spare our lives." Then the crew cast lots to see which of them had offended the gods and caused the terrible storm. When they did this, the lots identified Jonah as the culprit. "Why has this awful storm come down on us?" they demanded. "Who are you? What is your line of work? What country are you from? What is your nationality?" Jonah answered, "I am a Hebrew, and I worship the Lord, the God of heaven, who made the sea and the land." The sailors were terrified when they heard this, for he had already told them he was running away from the Lord. "Oh, why did you do it?" they groaned. And since the storm was getting worse all the time, they asked him, "What should we do to you to stop this storm?" "Throw me into the sea," Jonah said, "and it will become calm again. I know that this terrible storm is all my fault." Instead, the sailors rowed even harder to get the ship to the land. But the stormy sea was too violent for them, and they couldn't make it. Then they cried out to the Lord, Jonah's God. "O Lord," they pleaded, "don't make us die for this man's sin. And don't hold us responsible for his death. O Lord, you have sent this storm upon him for your own good reasons. Then the sailors picked Jonah up and threw him into the raging sea, and the storm stopped at once! The sailors were awestruck by the Lord's great power, and they offered him a sacrifice and vowed to serve him. Jonah 1:4-16 NLT*

Notice the impact Jonah's flight from God had on others. We fail to realize that when we run away from what God wants us to do, the impact can be seen and recognized by others often before we see it ourselves.

Notice when he was confronted, Jonah knew the storm was because of his choices. Even when he told the sailors what to do with him, they tried to row even harder. Finally, they realized they could not outmaneuver the storm, and as a last resort, they threw Jonah overboard. Can you imagine how they felt when the storm stopped?

Have you ever been in a boat in the middle of a storm? It is a frightening place to be! A few summers ago, I took a trip to northern Minnesota, to a place called the Boundary Waters with my two sons and a friend and his son. The Boundary Waters is a wilderness area where no motorized boats are allowed and you use a canoe to get to your camp sites. When we were at our camp site, a strong wind came up and made it difficult to go out on the lake. Each day the wind continued to blow and as we got closer to our day to leave, we were afraid the high winds would keep us on the island.

On the morning of our departure, the wind had not let up, but we needed to get out to return home. We did not have a way to communicate with our families to tell them we would be delayed and feared they would be worried if they did not hear from us. So we packed up our bags, loaded our canoes and headed out. Our first leg was a short paddle across the lake to our portage. The wind was in our face, but we made it and got across the portage for our second and final paddle to our destination.

When we got on the second and much larger lake, the wind was blowing stronger and the waves were larger. I was in the third canoe with my youngest son when we set out. The wind blew in our face and waves were spilling over the front and sides of the canoe. We got out about 100 yards and we could not go any further. We were paddling with all of our might, but we were not making any progress.

Paddling a canoe against high winds and heavy waves requires hard work and strength to keep the nose of the canoe directly into the wind and waves. Due to my inexperience, I was not able to do that and our canoe got sideways into the wind and waves. After what seemed like hours but was only minutes of struggle, our canoe rolled spilling us into the lake.

Fortunately, we were near a campsite and the wind pushed us ashore. We were able to empty the water from our canoe and set out again for our destination. Of course, having capsized once already, we were even more terrified by the wind and the waves.

We worked hard at keeping to the shoreline, pushing ourselves foot-by-foot along the way. However, every time we put our canoe out into the wind, hurricane gusts blew us right back to shore. We battled this wind and finally got around our first point.

As we entered the second bay, we saw a boat in front of us. This lake was just outside of the Boundary Waters, so motorized boats are allowed. That boat did not do anything to help us, but seeing the boat and knowing it was available to help us in an emergency gave us the strength to move forward and make it the remainder of the way to our landing. It was not easy, and the paddle out was the hardest and scariest experience I have ever faced, but we made it.

What does that story have to do with Jonah? When the sailors were in the storm and facing the winds and waves, it was Jonah's calm response and directions to throw him overboard that ultimately gave the sailor's hope, much like the boat in the lake was for me. When they took action, the storm stopped and they were saved.

Back to the purpose of the chapter, **when you ignore or run from God's plans, there will be consequences.** For me personally, I knew that God wanted me to do something different with my life, but I chose to put it off and wait for my timing. After praying the prayer of audacious faith, I laid "Sun Stand Still" aside. My work life took an eventful turn.

At work we had just installed a new application that managed how our business partners communicated with Target and it did not go well. Several errors were made and we ended up shutting down the pathway to communicate with our vendors. We were in crisis mode and my work life became 20-hour days working seven days a week.

This recovery process took six weeks and we worked hard to fix the problem and recover information that had been lost. It was the biggest storm I had faced in my career at Target. We made it through and I thought I was finally on the other side of the disaster. Little did I expect that on the morning of November 14th, 2011 my boss would meet with me to tell me that my career of 20 years at Target was over. Just like that, I was tossed overboard. God was in control, not me. He had others plans for me and He knew that without something drastic, I would continue to put off His plans.

I was thrown from my comfort zone! I had lost everything that I had known as normal. What would I do now?

REFLECTION QUESTIONS

- What have been some of the consequences in your life when you avoided God's calling on your life?

- Have you ever lost a job and felt like you were in a hopeless situation? What was your response and how did you see God working through that situation?

- How have your choices impacted the lives of those around you?

4 | EMOTIONS OF LOSS

Now the Lord had arranged for a great fish to swallow Jonah. And Jonah was inside the fish for three days and three nights. Jonah 1:17 NLT

God sent some type of sea animal to save Jonah. I am not sure that Jonah felt like it was saving him as he was being swallowed, but it was better than drowning, I guess. The Bible does not say what it was like inside the sea animal, but I am sure it was a place of darkness, fear and loneliness. Was he going to die in the belly of this animal? I can only imagine what it was like. But I do know that it must have been terrible because Jesus references Jonah's experience with his own death and resurrection:

One day some teachers of religious law and Pharisees came to Jesus and said, "Teacher, we want you to show us a miraculous sign to prove your authority." But Jesus replied, "Only an evil, adulterous generation would demand a miraculous sign; but the only sign I will give them is the sign of the prophet Jonah. For as Jonah was in the belly of the great fish for three days and three nights, so will the Son of Man be in the heart of the earth for three days and three nights." Matthew 12: 38-40 NLT

When I lost my job, not only had I lost my identity but also had lots of other emotions to overwhelm me. Maybe you have felt some of them in the past.

The first emotion was the sense of **abandonment**. When a job goes away, for whatever reason, you feel as if you have been cast away and abandoned. You feel rejected and so very alone.

Six years ago, in November of 2011 was my 20th anniversary with Target. For each anniversary, the company provides a gift based on the number of years of service and a card for peers to sign.

One of my greatest hurts was that during this process I was given my service award with an empty card, no encouraging remarks from my coworkers. My leaders, who were letting me go, could not even take the time to sign a card or say something nice about the twenty years I had given to Target. It re-enforced that feeling of abandonment. I was just being thrown away with no regard for what I had given to the company or the impact that I had made in the lives of those I worked with.

The second emotion I experienced was **loss of identity.** So much of who we are gets wrapped up in what we do. I was a Director at Target. My self-worth came from my title and the responsibilities that I had. When introduced to people, generally the first question asked is "What do you do?" When you lose a job, you lose your answer. You no longer have a title or position to go with your name. What do you say when you are unemployed? Learning who I am is one of the lessons that God had ahead for me. But more on that later.

The third emotion I felt was a **loss of control.** For me, this was probably the one that was the hardest. I was losing my income, my retirement, my way to pay for my kids' education, my comfort. All the things that I was holding on to and trying to plan for were gone. I thought that I had everything figured out. I thought I knew when I would retire, how much money I would have and what my next seven years would look like.

When you lose control, you lose your peace of mind. I had been comfortable and just going through the motions of life. As I would learn, this is a very dangerous place to be.

The fourth emotion I felt was **feelings of inadequacy**. I lost something that men may struggle with more than women, my position of being the provider for my family. I was raised in a very traditional Christian home where the man was to be the head of the household and the provider for his family. When you lose your job, your position in the family gets challenged and how you are to lead your family is under attack. I worked hard at my job and it provided a great salary that gave my family many blessings. Suddenly I had to deal with the reality that all of that was gone.

The fifth emotion I felt was the **loss of routine**. I had a pattern to my life. I got up early, went to work, came home for dinner with the family, spent the evening with them, caught up on work before going to bed and then did it all over the next day. This may sound terrible to some of you, but to me it was what I knew and what I liked. I liked knowing the plan and what the next day, week and month would look like.

The sixth and final emotion I felt from my job loss was **anger**. I was mad for the way I was treated. I was mad with the people who were instrumental in wanting me gone. I wanted to fight and prove that they were wrong, but I also knew that would change nothing and only make things worse in the long run. Maybe you can relate to that.

Whatever I go through, and maybe when you go through those difficult and challenging times, it is natural to experience a wide range of emotional swings and challenges. There is nothing wrong with experiencing emotions like these. The challenge for me was what do I do next?

How do I respond to these emotions? Where do I turn for help?

REFLECTION QUESTIONS

- If you have gone through some form of loss, what emotions and feelings did you go through?
- Who were you able to find to help you process through those emotions?
- What did you learn about yourself during this time?
- What did you learn that you can use to help others who are going through tough times?

5 | THE PRAYER

When you are in your moments of despair, how do you respond? Jonah was alone in the belly of a sea creature. It was dark, smelly and hard to see a way out. What did Jonah do? He prayed to God.

> *"Then Jonah prayed to the Lord his God from inside the fish. He said, "I cried out to the Lord in my great trouble, and He answered me. I called to You from the land of the dead, and Lord, You heard me! You threw me into the ocean depths, and I sank down to the heart of the sea. The mighty waters engulfed me; I was buried beneath Your wild and stormy waves. Then I said, 'O Lord, You have driven me from your presence. Yet I will look once more toward your holy Temple.' "I sank beneath the waves, and the waters closed over me. Seaweed wrapped itself around my head. I sank down to the very roots of the mountains. I was imprisoned in the earth, whose gates lock shut forever. But You, O Lord my God, snatched me from the jaws of death! As my life was slipping away, I remembered the Lord. And my earnest prayer went out to You in Your Holy Temple. Those who worship false gods turn their backs on all God's mercies. But I will offer sacrifices to You with songs of praise, and I will fulfill all my vows. For my salvation comes from the Lord alone." Then the Lord ordered the fish to spit Jonah out onto the beach." Jonah 2:1-10 NLT*

This prayer was both a prayer of despair and a prayer of hope. Jonah recognized where he was in life and that he was in trouble. He knew his only hope was God, which is often the case for people. They have to sink to the lowest point before they recognize their need for help, their need for God and a need to be rescued. Jonah had finally learned that his rescue could only come from God. Not man, not a job, not his family. No, his rescue and ours only comes from God.

When people suffer loss, so often they turn to other things to make them feel better rather than God. As mentioned in the prior chapter, people who have suffered loss are filled with emotions ranging from anger and bitterness to feelings of depression and fear. They often turn to drugs or alcohol to try to relieve the pain. They may turn to friends or family to help them get out of the pit. They look everywhere for help, but so often forget to turn to God to ask for help.

For me, my reaction to this loss was similar to how Jonah responded. He knew the reason for the storm was because he was running from God and the solution for those sailors was for him to be tossed overboard.

I knew that God wanted me to follow Him and do something different with my life. Losing my job was God's way of breaking the "Golden Handcuffs." These handcuffs were preventing me from hearing or responding to God's direction in my life. I was controlled by money, how much I made and how much was in my retirement account. There was no way that I had the faith to walk away from the financial security I had to live by faith and trust God to meet my financial needs in ministry. Or so I thought!

After that meeting with my boss, I went home from work and I journaled my thoughts. Here is what I wrote that afternoon:

~~~

> *What a day it has been. I had a one on one with my boss at 7:30. The meeting started with me putting away my notes and him telling me that we had to have a serious conversation. I knew what was coming next. He said that with all of the problems that I had recently experienced there was no support for me in my current position. I asked just my current area or anywhere and he said anywhere across Target Technical Services. He said my style was too abrasive and I did not build partners or confidence in my abilities.*
>
> *What a shocker. I knew something was not right, but I did not know what it was. I thought things were on the rebound, but I was wrong.*
~~~

Now the challenge is to figure out what to do with the rest of my life. How to pay for the kids' education, health insurance and just having a job.

Lots of things to work out. I left work as it was hard to control my emotions. I feel down. Like I have thrown 20 years of my life away. Part of me is angry, sad, hurt, numb.

I know that there must be a plan that God has for me in all of this. After all the hours I have spent for Target, you feel like you have been betrayed. Where is the loyalty?

Now comes the hard work. What am I going to do next? I am too young and don't have enough money to retire. I don't know what I want to do next – work in another corporate position, work in IT or operations, work in a non-profit or work in ministry. Maybe this was the only way that God could get my attention and look at the jobs that need me, but I would not have looked at because of what I would have to give up by leaving Target. Now that barrier is gone, I have to look to see if there is something else in His plan for me. Hard to see it now, but I know in time it will be revealed.

~~~

This journal entry was my prayer, just like Jonah's prayer. I knew that God had something for me and I was ready to do whatever that was going to be.

That night my children all came home to support me. My wife was in California with her parents visiting her brother, and my kids did not want me to be alone. We cried together that night, but it was a special time for them to show me that they loved me when I needed it most.
~~~

REFLECTION QUESTIONS

- What challenging experiences have you gone through in your life?
- How did you respond to the challenges?
- Who came around you to support you?
- Where did you turn for support? Were you able to turn to God for support or did you turn to the world around you?

6 | THE JOURNEY

God spoke to Jonah again:

> *"Then the Lord spoke to Jonah a second time: "Get up and go to the great city of Nineveh, and deliver the message I have given you." This time Jonah obeyed the Lord's command and went to Nineveh, a city so large that it took three days to see it all." Jonah 3:1-3 NLT*

We do not know a lot of details from the Bible about what happened after being spit up onto dry land. But we know that Jonah traveled to Nineveh to share God's message. Historians say that it is about a 30-day trip to Nineveh if traveled by foot, so Jonah had a lot of time to think about his calling while he walked.

One of the blessings of being without a job is the **gift of time**. You have time to think and dream and ask God about what is the next step in your life. Now you finally have time to sleep, time to reconnect with old friends, time with family and time to spend talking and listening to God. I talked to my brother-in-law Gary about his experience of being unemployed. He had lost his job after 40 years with a company. One of the things he learned and shared with me was to take some time and enjoy life. Don't get so focused on finding the next job that you miss out on the time you have been given. That was great advice.

As I reflected, taking time to connect with others and God and for me, this was something that I had not done well over the prior season of my life. I did not realize how exhausted I was and how my work was consuming my life. I was always working and my phone never left my side. I had been managing large teams in the US and in India and was working around the clock. I had gotten into a rhythm of sleeping four to five hours. I often wonder if I had not lost my job what staying at Target would have done to my health and if I could have continued to maintain that pace.

What I found as I started to have some free time was just how depleted my soul was. I had been so focused on my job that my soul had been ignored. I had not been taking time to talk to God and more importantly taking the time to listen to God. My family certainly noticed the signs of my emptiness but I did not see them. I thought I was doing a good job of keeping it all together.

Having time to reflect and listen to God and those around me taught me some really important lessons. These lessons became an important part of my faith journey and have played an important part in helping me navigate the next five years of my life. What I had just learned helped prepare me for what God was going to teach me in my next job, which you will hear more about later.

The first lesson that God taught me was that **He wants my whole heart**, not just part of it. God wanted all of me, not the small part I put Him in. What I learned about myself was that I had worked hard to compartmentalize everything in my life. I gave God His part, but then chose to use the rest of the compartments for myself. I gave my tithes, my service and my attendance at church, but then everything else belonged to me. I thought I was living my life for God in a good way, but I came to learn that God did not just want part of my heart, He wants all of it.

A second lesson I learned was to **take a risk.** I had been living my life within my own comfort zone. I was not willing to step outside of that comfort zone and see what God wanted to do through me. Here is what I wrote in my journal about a month after losing my job:

The devotional, "Jesus Calling" had this teaching for December 12th:

> *Be willing to go out on a limb with Me. If that is where I am leading you, it is the safest place to be. Your desire to live a risk-free life is a form of unbelief. Your longing to live close to Me is at odds with your attempts to minimize risk. You are approaching a crossroads in your journey. In order to follow Me wholeheartedly, you must relinquish your tendency to play it safe.*

Let Me lead you step by step through this day. If your primary focus is on Me, you can walk along perilous paths without being afraid. Eventually, you will learn to relax and enjoy the adventure of our journey together. As long as you stay close to Me, My sovereign Presence protects you wherever you go.[1]

In my journal I wrote these words in response:

~~~

What a great challenge for me. How am I demonstrating that I am willing to go out on a limb with God and be a risk taker. What does it mean to go out on a limb? What is taking a risk? Is it making yourself available for a position that does not exist, but that you know you could add value to the organization? Is it applying for a job that fits your skills, but is an environment that is totally different than what you have done before? Is it looking at jobs or opportunities that have eternal value, but pay significantly less than what you used to make? Is it moving to another state or country to serve Him?

God help me to be a risk taker in following You. Help me to listen to Your voice to hear what You want me to do with the skills and gifts You have given me. I don't know what that is, but help me to have an open mind and to listen to Your voice. You have sent messages to me letting me know You are in control. Help me to continue to listen to those messages.

I need to leave it in Your hands. I do not want to get so excited about an opportunity that if it does not work out I get disappointed and stop listening to You. But I also know that I have to take some risks to make those opportunities become a reality.

1 (Young 2008)
~~~

Thanks for this time to help me to lean on You. Thanks for Your promises to take care of us and to provide for us. Thanks for the hope You give me of not only this life but more importantly the future we have in You and eternity in heaven. Help me to hear Your voice and follow You in Your plan for my life.

~~~

A third lesson I learned was **don't wait to tell people what they mean to you**. When you leave a job that you have had for a long time, it is a lot like a funeral. What you knew as normal and what you have done for years is gone: co-workers, routine, status.

As you leave that company or when you are gone, people may share with you the impact that you made on their lives, but so often we never share those kind words with the people whom we are currently working. Here was my journal entry reflecting on this:

~~~

When I left Target, I received many notes and emails from people I had worked with over the past twenty years sharing with me the impact that I had made in their lives. The comments over and over affirmed that God has given me the ability to lead teams, develop people and connect value with the work that people do.

The comments came in three simple words - ***engage, inspire and empower.*** *I feel God leading me to use these three simple words to do the impossible.*

~~~

A fourth lesson I learned was **how amazing God's timing is**. As I mentioned earlier in the book, after attending the Leadership Summit I started reading "Sun Stand Still." I had read the first eight chapters, but then I had put it down and had not read any more. After leaving Target I picked up the book again and finished reading it. I realized that I had not been ready to hear what God wanted to say to me in the remaining chapters. God knew that I would need
~~~

to read this after losing my job to encourage, inspire and challenge me for whatever would come next. Here was my journal entry capturing some of the highlights from the book:

~~~

This morning I started reading "Sun Stand Still" again from Steven Furtick. I had started reading the book after the Leadership Summit, but had put it down a couple of months ago and had not read it since. The chapter I started with today was about a simple theology - God is Great, God is Good!

Under God is Great, the book said "Dream God-worthy dreams. Pray faith fueled prayers. Live a life that can be explained only by the existence of a God who is infinitely great." "If your problem is too big for you, it's just the right size for God."[2]

Under God is Good, the book said, "Knowing God is great enables you to dream, pray and live beyond your means because you know He is able to respond. But knowing God is also good enables you to dream, pray, and live beyond your means because you know He wants to respond."[3]

The chapter ended with this comment: "Build your confidence in His goodness and His greatness, and He will do the impossible. In our day, in your life. For His glory." [4]

~~~

2 (Furtick, Sun stand still: what happens when you dare to ask God for the impossible 2010, 99)
3 (Furtick, Sun stand still: what happens when you dare to ask God for the impossible 2010, 102)
4 (Furtick, Sun stand still: what happens when you dare to ask God for the impossible 2010, 107)

After reading this chapter, I wanted to go back and read the chapter before to see where I had left off. That chapter was the "Surcharge of Sacrifice. It talked about the sacrifice of Joshua and the personal sacrifice you have to make to do something amazing, as he said "Trade off to Trade up."

> *There's always a trade-off. Before God can bring His promises to pass in your life, He has to strip away all the stuff that keeps you from trusting Him wholeheartedly." "Crossing over into God's promise is always accompanied by a cutting-away process." and it continued: "The things that God will call you to lay down or walk away from will depend a lot on where you've come from and where He's taking you."*[5]

The book continued with the story of a corporate leader who was fired due to his decision to do what was right and not lie. He lost his job, but took this opportunity to take on a job leading a mission area that is sending a thousand people to help dig wells in a foreign land. The following words hit me hard:

> *"But God stepped in and initiated a divine downsize." "Now he realizes that when God removes something from our lives, it's not because he's trying to take away something good. It's because he's trying to make room for something better."*[6]

> *"It's a trade-off. It will definitely cost you something. But it's always a trade-up. Why? Because God always gives back so much more than He takes away. When He takes something or someone out of our life, He's just clearing space in your hard drive for an update."*[7]

---

5 (Furtick, Sun stand still: what happens when you dare to ask God for the impossible 2010, 85)
6 (Furtick, Sun stand still: what happens when you dare to ask God for the impossible 2010, 87)
7 (Furtick, Sun stand still: what happens when you dare to ask God for the impossible 2010, 88)

These comments hit me right where I was that day. I felt that leaving Target was a "Divine Downsizing" and God was preparing me for something amazing. This verse was very meaningful for me:

> *No discipline in enjoyable while it is happening – it's painful! But afterward there will be a peaceful harvest of right living for those who are trained in this way. Hebrews 12:11 NLT*

"Sun Stand Still" then talked about the story of Joseph.

> *"Don't let anybody but God Himself put you in your place. And don't stop forging ahead when you encounter opposition. The fact that you're fighting big battles means that you're close to even bigger blessings. The reason you're facing fierce resistance now is that God is preparing an astonishing reward in your future."* [8]

> *"He's aligning your desires with His desires so that He can accomplish the impossible in your life. And once you've made up your mind to pay the price and to trust the Lord with all your heart, no level of spiritual achievement is out of reach. Because when you want what God wants for the reasons He wants it, you're unstoppable."*[9]

It ended with a pledge:

> *"By God's grace, no matter what it costs me, I'm going to live by audacious faith. I'm going to believe God for the impossible, to accomplish by and for Him what I cannot accomplish on my own. No matter what people think about my vision for my life, I'm going to take God at His word. I'm going to trust Him with my whole heart and follow Him step by step, even when my surrender requires sacrifice. Even if it seems like He's taken me over the edge, I will trust that He'll be there to catch me if I fall. I will trust that He is good and that somehow, someday, He will work all things in my life together for my good and His glory." 10*

8 (Furtick, Sun stand still: what happens when you dare to ask God for the impossible 2010, 91)
9 (Furtick, Sun stand still: what happens when you dare to ask God for the impossible 2010, 92)
10 (Furtick, Sun stand still: what happens when you dare to ask God for the impossible 2010, 92)

This was the last chapter I read when I started the book. Why did I stop after this pledge? Was it God prompting me to wait to read about the action steps until after I was ready to move forward with the pledge? I found myself crying as I thought how God worked these together. The Leadership Summit and this book began the process of moving me to consider something other than Target.

In my journal on September 18th I wrote the following prayer:

~~~

God give me the faith to do great things for You. Help me to know what You want me to do that I can only do because of You and with Your help!

~~~

The next thing I knew, God began the process of answering my prayer by removing my "Golden Handcuffs" at Target and the tradeoff process began. Then after the past three weeks of beginning the "trade-up" process, God prompted me to pick up the book and it was the perfect chapter to begin to move my process forward. I wrote the following in my journal:

~~~

What is the impossible that God wants to do through me? *I feel God leading me in a direction. I find myself thinking about some pretty impossible things that only He could do, but I would sure be excited to be part of. I am finding the people around me affirming this direction in my life by their suggestions and thoughts. Could I be at the beginning stage of being part of helping an organization do some impossible things that are truly God sized. Has God been preparing me the past 20 years for a role that can use the gifts He has given me to do something impossible?*

~~~

The final lesson that God taught me during this time was to **trust God more**. Trust is one of those things that Christians talk about, but for me it is something that I struggle with. It is easy to say you are trusting God when things are going great in your life, but is that really trust?

It is when I am going through hardships that I really know where my trust level is. Losing your job and not knowing where your next paycheck is going to come from provided an opportunity to learn a lesson in trust. Being patient and waiting for God to provide according to His plans is hard to do. If you are like me, you want to grab the first thing that comes along, but that can be the wrong decision. You can go through countless interviews and rejections and begin to wonder when God will provide. You may have to adjust your spending levels to reflect the loss of income or the fact that the next job may pay less, as I did. Like me, you learn to trust that God will help in putting all the pieces together.

What I learned is that when you put it in God's hands, He does provide, but you have to do your part. You have to spend the time talking and listening to God and rebuilding that relationship. Then you have to follow up on the leads and contacts that He gives you and you have to be patient. God does not always move at the speed or pace that we want Him to.

God provided leads the week my position at Target ended. God connected me with Eagle Brook Church and I began the process of interviewing and determining if this was where God wanted me to be. He provided other leads, but as some doors closed, it became clear that Eagle Brook was the destination that He had planned for me. I was hired and started in my new role as Executive Director of Campus Ministries. This was my calling and this is where God would begin the next season of molding and shaping me.

REFLECTION QUESTIONS

- When you have gone through a season of change, what did God teach you and what did you learn?

- How did God show up in amazing ways to help and support you?

- When control was taken away from you, how did you learn to trust God more?

7 | THE CALLING

Jonah completed his journey and was now ready to fulfill the purpose of his calling. He was there to tell the people of Nineveh to change their ways and follow God.

> *On the day Jonah entered the city, he shouted to the crowds: "Forty days from now Nineveh will be destroyed!" The people of Nineveh believed God's message, and from the greatest to the least, they declared a fast and put on burlap to show their sorrow. When the king of Nineveh heard what Jonah was saying, he stepped down from his throne and took off his royal robes. He dressed himself in burlap and sat on a heap of ashes. Then the king and his nobles sent this decree throughout the city: "No one, not even the animals from your herds and flocks, may eat or drink anything at all. People and animals alike must wear garments of mourning, and everyone must pray earnestly to God. They must turn from their evil ways and stop all their violence. Who can tell? Perhaps even yet God will change his mind and hold back his fierce anger from destroying us." When God saw what they had done and how they had put a stop to their evil ways, he changed his mind and did not carry out the destruction he had threatened. Jonah 3:4 -10* NLT

This proclamation to humble themselves before God resulted in the people of Nineveh changing their ways and avoiding God's judgement. History tells us that the city prospered for another 150 years after this change before they were destroyed by the Babylonians in 612 BC.

There are some really important lessons for all of us from this passage of the Bible.

First, **God loves all people.** The Assyrians were the enemies of Israel and were oppressing the people of that day, yet God wanted to save them if they would follow Him and His ways.

We all need to get better at loving people who are not like us. It is much easier to love those who look like us, talk like us and share similar values as us, but what about people who are raised in different cultures, lifestyles or religious backgrounds? Do we really show them we love them? I know for myself, it is easier to judge other people for how they look, dress or appear and never take the time to learn to love them for who they are as children of God. God wants us as Christ followers to love those around us in the same way that He loves the world.

Second, **if you accept God's grace through Jesus Christ you will be saved and your sins will be forgiven.** God changed his plans to destroy Nineveh because they repented and changed their ways. God will do the same for every person who accepts His grace through Jesus Christ, no matter what you have done in your life! We are all born as sinners and none of us deserve the grace that God offers, but it is available for all. We just have to accept it and allow God to enter into our life.

Third, **share the message of God's love for us** to others. God gave instructions directly to Jonah and in Matthew, Jesus challenged His disciples:

> *"Jesus came and told his disciples, "I have been given all authority in heaven and on earth. Therefore, go and make disciples of all the nations, baptizing them in the name of the Father and the Son and the Holy Spirit. Teach these new disciples to obey all the commands I have given you. And be sure of this: I am with you always, even to the end of the age."" Matthew 28:18-20 NLT*

There is no greater purpose in life than to work toward reaching the people of this world who need God's forgiveness and salvation.

As I completed my journey and decided what job I would do next in my career, I wanted to work for an organization that had a purpose that aligned with what God was directing me towards. I spent the time I was given on my journey to reflect and identify my own purpose and the values that I wanted to aspire to in the next phase of my life.

I put it into a model so that it was easy for me to remember. Here it is:

The Post 4P Model

Purpose
Passions
Principles
Practices

PURPOSE - This is probably the mission of the organization that you might work for. If you don't believe in the purpose, it will be hard for you to be "all in" and you will not be as motivated and fulfilled doing your job.

The Purpose is about aligning your passions, principles and practices (who you are) with what you do and who you do it for.

For 20 years I aligned my passions, principles and practices with the purpose of Target. I believed in the values that Target held and I was able to contribute to its purpose.

However, I am now much more driven to align who I am with a new purpose, which I feel God is leading me towards. I felt God was leading me to work for His purpose and find an organization that needs my Passions, Principles and Practices to help it achieve its Purpose.

Life is too short to spend your time doing things that don't align who you are with what you do.

PASSIONS - What are your passions? What do you love to do and find you never get tired when you are doing these things? My passion is to coach and develop people to become a better representation of themselves: Spiritually, emotionally, intellectually and professionally. This takes the shape of engaging, inspiring and empowering people whom I interact with. Passions are your motivation.

PRINCIPLES - These are the standards that you try to operate by. As I have led teams and gained experience, I have adopted these principles as my guiding areas of focus. My five personal leadership principles include the following:

1. Create a team that people want to be part of.

2. Have open and honest communication - operate with a welcome policy that encourages anyone to talk about whatever is on their heart.

3. Development is a high priority – always focus on helping the person to improve themselves – spiritually, emotionally, intellectually and professionally.

4. Do it first, do it best – though we are not all called to lead an organization or even part of an organization, we are called to model Christlikeness so others can learn from that model. So do your job with efficiency and high quality.

5. Maintain work life balance - create an environment that helps people be well rounded in all aspects of their lives: work, social, spiritual, emotional, physical.

PRACTICES - These are your skills or talents that you bring to the table. "Strengths Based Leadership"[1] is a book that can help with this if you do not know what your strengths are. Through that book, I learned that my strengths include the following:

---

1 (Rath, Tom; Conchie, Barry 2009)

1. Relator – enjoy close relationships with others and find deep satisfaction in working hard with friends to achieve a goal.

2. Strategic – create alternative ways to proceed and faced with any given scenario, they can quickly spot the relevant patterns and issues.

3. Responsibility – take ownership of what they say they will do and are committed to stable values such as honesty and loyalty.

4. Analytical – search for reasons and causes and have the ability to think about all the factors that might affect a situation.

5. Maximizer – focus on strengths as a way to stimulate personal and group excellence and seek to transform something strong into something superb.

Some of the other strengths explained in the book include: Achiever, Arranger, Belief, Consistency, Deliberative, Discipline, Focus, Restorative, Activator, Command, Communication, Competition, Self-Assurance, Significance, Woo, Adaptability, Developer, Connectedness, Empathy, Harmony, Includer, Individualization, Positivity, Context, Futuristic, Ideation, Input, Intellection and Learner. If you do not know what your strengths are, I highly recommend purchasing this book and taking the assessment to learn what your primary strengths are.

I was hired by Eagle Brook Church as the Executive Director of Campus Ministries in March 2012. I had been without a job for four months and I was ready to begin the ministry that I believe God prepared for me.

As I started my new job, I wrote this prayer:

~~~

God - Why Me?

Of all the people you could have selected to work for your church, why me? What do you see in the future that You needed me to leave my old job for?

What God sized happening do You need me for that is worth the sacrifice of what I gave up? What did You see in me that needed to change?

Why me? I don't have a background in ministry or training in the Bible.

Why me? I don't have experience as a pastor or the ability to teach in front of a crowd. What did You see that I don't? Did you just want me for Yourself?

I don't understand what happened, I don't understand why You wanted me, but I know that You have something big for me. When Jesus called the disciples to follow Him, I wonder did they ask "why me"? They were not the educated religious leaders or the popular people, but look what You accomplished through them!

What are You going to accomplish through me? When so many people ask for Your guidance, but You are silent, why did You speak so clearly to me?

Why me?

When You removed the golden handcuffs of my former employer was it to see how I would respond? Would I seek Your plan for my life or look for something to replace the income that I lost? Have I
~~~

learned to trust You and rely on Your strength and guidance or do I try to accomplish things from my own strength?

As I move forward in my new job, may this be my daily prayer:

Help me to be humble and open to coaching and feedback. Help me to not push on things that are not needed to be pushed on, while also not allowing things that are just good enough to be ignored.

May my heart be seen in all that I do and may my motives for change be pure and be led by seeking Your purpose and plan.

Help me to lead as You would lead.

Help we to coach as You would coach.

Help me to inspire and motivate as You would inspire and motivate.

Help me to serve as You would serve.

Help me to love as You would love.

Thank you for this opportunity and may I be about accomplishing Your purposes in all that I do.

Help me to be part of accomplishing things that can only be accomplished by You through me.

Amen!

~~~
~~~

REFLECTION QUESTIONS

- What has God called you to do? If you don't know, have you asked God about it?
- Who are the people that you need to tell about God's love for them?
- What are your strengths and passions? How are you using them to accomplish your purpose?
- Who are the people that you find hard to love? What can you do to change your heart and share God's love with them?

8 | MY STORY

As I said earlier, we do not know much about Jonah other than he was a prophet whose father was Amittai and was from the town of Gath-Hepher. Jonah began his time as a prophet around 793 BC and goes to Nineveh around 759 BC. Jonah's ministry ends in 753 BC, around six years after going to Nineveh. The King of Assyria was Ashur-Dan III during this time.

We don't have a lot of details about Jonah, but I have a little more that I can add about myself. This will help set the stage for who I was when I started my role at Eagle Brook and what God had ahead for me.

I was the youngest of five children and there was a six-year spread between me and my closest sibling. My father was a pastor who served in small Baptist churches in small communities in Minnesota, Iowa and Wisconsin. My mom was a part-time nurse in the local hospital and supported my dad by volunteering at the churches where he was a pastor.

I was raised in a very traditional, conservative Baptist home, which meant attending every church service and following all of the rules. My parents loved their children and provided for us the best they could with the little money they had. We knew that we were loved, but we were not an affectionate family who hugged each other or said I love you on a regular basis. In many respects, I would say that I felt like I had to earn their love by my behavior.

I made the decision to accept Jesus Christ as my Savior when I was seven-years-old with my mom next to her bed one evening. I was baptized when I was 12 and, I am fortunate to say that I have known Jesus as my Savior for most of my life.

However, I would say that my faith was more of a set of rules and head knowledge for most of my life until 2000 when I was 37 years-old. I knew what I believed and why I believed it and I did the things that good Christians do: I went to church and Sunday school, gave my tithes and volunteered to help where needed. As a boy, that meant mowing the grass, shoveling the snow and singing in the choir.

My parents moved to south Minneapolis when I was a fifth grader. This provided quite the culture shock after living in a small town of 1000 in Iowa. During middle and high school, I attended Minnehaha Academy, a private Christian school, where I received a great education and spiritual training.

In the middle of my junior year, my parents moved to New Richmond, Wisconsin to pastor a church there. I started at a new school where I knew nobody in the middle of that year.

Fortunately, a family back in Minnesota, from Minnehaha, offered to let me live with them my senior year, so I was able to return to Minnehaha and graduate with my friends. For all practical purposes I had moved out of my home at 16 and would never return to live under my parents' roof again.

The following year I started at Bethel College at 17 and graduated from there four years later. My parents did not have the money to put me through school so thanks to scholarships, loans and hard work I was able to put myself through and graduated with a degree in Business with an emphasis in Accounting.

In the winter of my senior year, I started dating my future wife, Beth Sahlin. We were engaged in December 1984 and married on December 28th, 1985.

There was nothing extraordinary about my high school and college years. I was not a star athlete, top student or class president, but I had some good friends that hung together. I was the classic do just enough to not be at the bottom but not so much to be at the top. I worked 30 – 40 hours a week while going to school full time and studied as much as I needed.

When I graduated, I was not blessed with job offers from great companies in the Twin Cities. Though I sent out 30 – 40 resumes, I got the same number of rejections. Because I needed a full-time job, I finally started working full time for IC System, Inc. as a bill collector. I put my hard-earned college degree to work calling people to pay their past due medical and credit card bills. What a way to start my career off!

However, as I look back, that job taught me some skills that have helped me throughout my career. I learned how to listen to what people were saying. Nobody wants to talk to a bill collector on the phone, but by listening to what they say to you, I was able to determine things like: why they did not pay in the first place, how much they could pay now or if they were never going to pay no matter what I did.

In a few months, I became the top collector in volume of calls and money collected. My hard work resulted in getting my supervisor to recommend me to a friend of hers who was a manager of collections at US Bank. After 15 months of working at IC System, I moved to US Bank to be a collection agent for their credit cards. I was still a bill collector, but it felt like a step up.

I worked in collections for 12 months and was promoted to a phone agent at First Financialine, still at US Bank. This moved me from dealing with people who did not want to talk to with me, to people who were calling about questions, and I could help them. It really was a sales job, as our goal was to help people open accounts over the phone rather than having to come into a branch. This was all before the internet and all of the on-line banking services.

Twelve months of this job allowed me to interview for the Internal Audit Training Program. This was a twenty-four-month program that trained people in various aspects of auditing for the bank. Finally, I was doing a job that used my college degree and accounting background. I spent time learning and doing branch audits, commercial loan audits and Electronic Data Processing audit.

This ended up being where I excelled the most and at the end of my training I was placed in the EDP audit department. During this time, I completed my CPA certification and my CISA (Certified Information System Auditing) certification. I assumed that I would have a long career in front of me at US Bank and in auditing, but that would not be the case.

At the time, US Bank was going through some difficult financial times and there were layoffs and consolidations. In June of 1991, the audit department was pulled into a meeting to tell us that our jobs were being outsourced to an external accounting firm. All but

12 positions were being eliminated. Six would stay to assist with commercial loan audits and the other six were being placed in other jobs at US Bank. I was one of those six and I was placed in an accounting position.

I had no options. I could take this job or be unemployed as I was not eligible for the severance package that the rest of the auditors received. I started my new job, but quickly learned that the department did not have work for me to do. I had a 40 hour a week job with 10 hours of work to do. It made for very long and boring days.

Three months later I received a call from Target. They were looking to hire an EDP auditor and one of my peers from US Bank had recommended me. They asked if I was interested in interviewing for the position. I said yes, and one week later I was offered the position at Target.

That was the end of my five years at US Bank, but those five years prepared me in many ways for the next 20 years at Target. I learned communication, accounting, audit and IT skills. I had opportunities to work on some big strategic projects and did some operational reviews of bank processes. I was able to complete some certifications which provided credentials for future jobs I would have, all helpful in my new position.

I started my Target career as an Information Systems Auditor in October of 1991.

With each job change came an increase in salary and responsibility. I spent 12 months in the audit role before I was promoted to a Financial Analyst in the Merchandise Presentation Department. Working in audit gave me a great opportunity to learn about Target and see all areas of the company. I was given opportunities to do some operational reviews and learn about the data structure of the corporation and how to use reporting tools to extract and analyze data.

During the next 19 years I had many different jobs at Target. I worked in Merchandise Presentation, Store Operations and Information Technology. I had wide ranging responsibilities doing analytics, operations, systems development and team management. I led teams ranging from two people to an organization with 400+ people.

During my time at Target, I was also able to create or develop several innovative processes that had been used for many years or are still around today. These included the following:

- Aisle numbering - This process linked merchandise to locations in the store, a process which is still used today for guest assistance, gift registry and pushing merchandise from the trucks to the sales floor.

- Prototype analysis - This was used to help allocate category space in stores as changes in remodels or designs were made.

- Sales and inventory reporting – Used to track productivity of sales by category, aisle or endcap by looking at inventory and sales. It was the first store specific instock reporting used to determine if there was sufficient inventory on the shelf to be in stock for the guest.

- Store Operational Scorecard - Used to evaluate store performance and assist leaders when visiting a store.

- Planogram Optimization - Part of team that developed a process to place products on a shelf using an optimization engine that we received a patent for.

My final role at Target was Information Technology Director and I was responsible for Merchandising and Supply Chain systems. I oversaw a department that had 400 to 500 employees and contractors and an annual budget of $60-70 million. In many ways, I felt that I had arrived at the pinnacle of success. I had status as a Director for Target with my own office and my own Administrative Assistant. It was from this level of corporate success that God called me to do His work.

During this time of professional accomplishments, our family was growing. My wife Beth had graduated from Bethel with an education degree. She was a fourth-grade teacher until our first son Justin, was born in April of 1990 and she chose to stay at home with him and not return to full time teaching. Our daughter Kala was born in October of 1991 and our youngest son Colin was born in February of 1993.

Beth was a stay-at-home mom until God started to nudge her to use her experience and begin working in ministry. She started back in a limited part-time role doing women's ministries with the Minnesota Baptist Conference in 1999, and then added part time work in children's ministries at Trinity Baptist Church. In 1993 she began her work with Love Lift for Ukraine and began leading teams to Ukraine to do summer day camps for kids and other women's ministries conferences.

We attended Sunday School and had great interactions with a group of friends our age. I served on the board at the church and also served as church chair during a season of change at the church.

We felt we were doing everything the right way. We were involved at church, generous with our tithes and raising our family. I worked a lot of hours, but I was also able to make getting home for dinner every night with my family a priority. I had the flexibility at work to attend any special event for our kids and Beth was very involved in raising the kids. We were like the All American Christian family! But something was missing!

We enjoyed our time with friends at church, but we were not being challenged to grow in our faith. We were not being pushed out of our comfort zone. Church felt like it was for people like us and we were not being challenged to minister to people needing Jesus. We were going through the motions but something was missing. At work, I was known as a church attending family man, but I did not outwardly share my faith with others. There was no fire to reach others for Christ.

In many ways, it looked like we were living the Christian life, but we were lacking the joy and peace that comes from the fruit of the spirit. In 1999, we started trying to push for some changes at church to be more seeker friendly, but we got frustrated pushing for change and felt alone in our desire. Eventually, we decided it was time for us to find a new church.

Changing churches is a lot like changing jobs. It means finding a new routine, new friends, and a new comfort zone. After checking out a couple of places, we landed at Eagle Brook Church. At that time, they met on a single campus in White Bear Lake, Minnesota. Immediately we sensed something was different. We heard messages that challenged us and that we discussed after we left. The music was more relevant and enjoyable. They had a Saturday night service so we started attending on Saturdays and that eliminated the battle to get the kids going on Sunday morning. Our kids actually wanted to go to church.

We met new friends and got involved in adult classes. But what was really different was that the pastors spoke about their own lives and their own struggles with living a Christian life. It felt like we were being brought along on a journey rather than being told what we should do. Things started to feel more about a relationship with Jesus Christ and less about the rules to follow. Gradually I started to feel a sense of wanting to reach my friends and neighbors for Christ instead of feeling embarrassed to invite others to church.

We got involved serving in kids' ministry and in 2002, Beth joined the staff at Eagle Brook Church. She served in this role for eight-and-a-half years. I helped her out in the program and also was involved in small group ministry and served on the nominating committee for the church board. We got involved in a small group and we did life together. We got together almost weekly and we traveled to Mexico, the Grand Canyon and the Boundary Waters together. God was working on us and preparing us for what happened in 2011.

So now you know my history. The next chapter of the book will talk about what happened next!

REFLECTION QUESTIONS

- How has your life experiences shaped your life?
- How did friends and/or family shape your feelings towards God?
- What is church to you? A place for family or a place to invite lost friends?
- How have you gotten involved in your church?

9 | MISSING THE POINT

Jonah brought God's message, the people responded, changed their ways and you would think that Jonah would be happy, but far from it. See how he responded:

> *"This change of plans greatly upset Jonah, and he became very angry. So he complained to the Lord about it: "Didn't I say before I left home that You would do this, Lord? That is why I ran away to Tarshish! I knew that You are a merciful and compassionate God, slow to get angry and filled with unfailing love. You are eager to turn back from destroying people. Just kill me now, Lord! I'd rather be dead than alive if what I predicted will not happen." The Lord replied, "Is it right for you to be angry about this?" Then Jonah went out to the east side of the city and made a shelter to sit under as he waited to see what would happen to the city. And the Lord God arranged for a leafy plant to grow there, and soon it spread its broad leaves over Jonah's head, shading him from the sun. This eased his discomfort, and Jonah was very grateful for the plant. But God also arranged for a worm! The next morning at dawn the worm ate through the stem of the plant so that it withered away. And as the sun grew hot, God arranged for a scorching east wind to blow on Jonah. The sun beat down on his head until he grew faint and wished to die. "Death is certainly better than living like this!" he exclaimed. Then God said to Jonah, "Is it right for you to be angry because the plant died?" "Yes," Jonah retorted, "even angry enough to die!" Jonah 4: 1 – 9 NLT*

Jonah suffered from **a heart and attitude problem**. Jonah never really had a love for the people of Nineveh. He brought God's message because he was told to (and went through a bit of an experience along the way). My guess was that Jonah had a great dislike or even hatred for the people of Nineveh. They were the enemies of Israel and not part of God's people, and Jonah

needed to have a change in his heart. But he also had an attitude issue.

When God decided to change His mind and not destroy Nineveh because of their change of heart, Jonah got mad. He had not gotten what he wanted and now he just wanted to die. His motivation for obedience was all wrong. He really wanted to see the people judged and destroyed.

He had given the message as he was told, but it was not what he really wanted to see happen.

There is a really important message in this that I don't want you to lose. **God's plans are always greater than our efforts and plans**. Being obedient, Jonah's message was still used to accomplish God's purpose, even when his attitude and heart were not behind the message. God is bigger than any of us.

This portion of Jonah also relates to my experience in living out my calling to work at Eagle Brook Church. In the back of my mind, and probably many others, when you take a job working at a church, there will be no problems. Everyone will welcome you with open arms, with complete trust and follow you wherever you lead them. Nice idea, but far from reality.

Yes, I was called by God to work at Eagle Brook Church, but God was far from done fixing me. I started my job with an attitude issue. I came in thinking that God had brought me to Eagle Brook Church to fix it, but, in reality, God brought me to Eagle Brook Church to **fix me**.

Over my five years on staff as an Executive Director, I had many challenges and mistakes that I had to overcome. Like the story of Jonah, God still did great things through Eagle Brook Church while I was there, but I had some fixing that needed to happen.

Over my five years, there were three significant things that God needed to remake. I was the lump of clay and God was using my experiences during these five years to make me into the vessel He wanted me to become.

The first thing that had to be remade was my **character**. I did not see these flaws in my character as they were clearly blind spots.

These things were not intentional flaws meant to hurt or harm, but they were issues that forced me to spend time in reflection to determine who I really was.

Nine months into my time at Eagle Brook, I was placed on a performance plan. I did not see this as a good thing because a performance plan is generally the last step before being let go and was meant to get your attention that change is needed immediately. It certainly did that! I never saw it coming and my first reaction was to turn in my resignation as I clearly was failing in doing my job.

My resignation was not accepted and I was encouraged to work the plan and begin the process of fixing my character issues. These were issues around the line between confidence and arrogance with perception or intent. My performance plan stated that I had caused problems in the following areas and they put it this way:

> *Manipulation, lack of trust and inconsistent follow-through – I manipulate situations or misrepresent others to advance my ideas or agenda. Intentionally going behind people's backs and not upfront with my intent. I am not interested in others' ideas. I represent that others are in alignment or agreement when they are not.*

> *Respect for others – expressed frustration (verbally and physically) in ways that others felt like anger was directed at them in intimidating manner and were afraid or uncomfortable. Discussed opinions of people in a way that was not honoring to them of God.*

> *Arrogance, lack of Humility – ask for thoughts and ideas and then ignored them or disregarded their input or ideas. My idea was the best and only option. Shut people down without fully hearing their ideas or thoughts. People are hesitant to confront or share ideas because they will be dismissed or talked down to. Lack of authentic humility and respect.*

I sat in stunned silence as the list was read to me. As a person who is a high achiever, who almost never had a negative performance review in his career and who chose a ministry job at a church over working in the corporate world, hearing these words devastated me.

Beyond the words, the thing that made this even harder was that there were no specifics of what I had done or to whom I had done them. No one had come to me to tell me how I was acting, they just told my boss.

I thought things between my team and me were going well, when in fact they really did not like working for or with me. Some of this may have been work culture differences, as I moved from a corporate world that stressed direct communication, to a church culture, but, in reality, most was about me. People knew about me but didn't really know my heart or motives and often would assume the worst.

So, what did I do? **I worked the plan**! I met with each person that had told my boss things about me and I asked for forgiveness. I tried to learn to recognize behaviors and actions I was doing and tried to change what I was doing. I tried to slow down, take more time to listen, ask questions and not make as many statements. I met with a professional counselor to explore the reason behind my behaviors so I could learn how to change them.

I enlisted a couple of confidants whom I could trust and asked them to hold me accountable, watch me in meetings or other interactions and tell me if they saw these behaviors. I wanted to be aware of when I did things that offended people at the time, so that I could learn how to readjust what and how I did things. I discovered that my dark side was often an overuse of one of my strengths. I had to learn to better balance my strengths with some other skills.

At the end of 90 days, my boss felt that I had made satisfactory progress and decided to remove me from the performance plan and not terminate me. The next year was a hard year working to rebuild my character and establish trust with those who did not trust me. It is hard work to show people that you are a different person when you have hurt or mistreated them in the past. It does not happen overnight, but these issues did not resurface again during my time at Eagle Brook thankfully.

The second issue that I needed to fix was my **chemistry.** After going through some staff members leaving from the executive team, some financial challenges that resulted in some layoffs and a major staff restructuring, our board felt it was time to bring in some professional help for the executive team. Part of this work included a survey about the executive team and about ourselves as members of that team.

The results were not encouraging and they pointed out many things that we needed to work on as a team and as individuals. Coming out of the meeting, I had a sense that the issues were really mine and that I was the major cause of our chemistry issues.

Once again, I asked if I should resign and I really began to wonder if this was really where God wanted me. I was assured by my boss that this was where God wanted me and that I was needed here. I also asked God to really make it clear if He wanted me to stay. As Gideon put a fleece before God to know God's intentions to attack the Midianites, I also put a fleece before God. To read the full story of Gideon and his fleece, read Judges six.

Specifically, my fleece was that I asked God to have someone send me unsolicited comments of support and encouragement. Within 24 hours I had received two specific emails that answered my request to God.

God answered that request in a personal and powerful way and assured me this is where He wanted me. Of course, that was because He was not yet done remaking me.

I began a personal quest to find the key factors that resulted in my chemistry issues. As a team, we worked through steps found in "Return on Character" by Fred Kiel. His book states that his research has found that there are four key areas that make up our character. They are Integrity, Responsibility, Forgiveness and Compassion.

The survey was sent to Eagle Brook Church employees asking about how the Executive Team rated in each of these categories. The results showed that I had opportunities to grow in all four areas, but that my biggest opportunities were in the forgiveness and compassion side.

I read through many books looking for help, and I found five books that made the biggest impact on me.

The first book was "Soul Keeping"[1] by John Ortberg. The second was "Crash the Chatterbox" [2] by Steven Furtick. The third book was "The end of me"[3] by Kyle Idelman. The fourth book was "Unqualified"[4] by Steven Furtick.

The final book, and the one that has made the greatest impact on me and helped me understand what God needed to reveal and heal in remaking me, was "Wild at Heart"[5] by John Eldredge. Reading this book really helped me to look into my past to try and understand what influenced me to be who I was, and what did I need to change, to create a better version of myself. Here is my journal reflecting in what God taught me from this book:

~~~

This book is about finding out who we are as men and what true masculinity looks like. It started by saying we all have three things that are the center of our soul:

We want a battle to fight.

We want an adventure to live.

We want a beauty to rescue

The basis of this book is that true masculinity is the image of God that comes out in all of us and that through the fall of mankind, we have all lost our focus on being able to understand and live this out. It talks about how we all need a father to teach us these things and how many of us have not had these things taught to us by our fathers.

---

1 (Ortberg 2014)

2 (Furtick, Crash the Chatterbox: Hearing God's Voice Above All Others 2015)

3 (Idelman 2015)

4 (Furtick, (Un)qualified: how God uses broken people to do big things 2016)

5 (Eldredge 2006)
~~~

Ultimately, God is our Father, but through our wounds we have failed to see and be filled by God the Father. we all have a wound that needs to be recognized and healed. It made me ask some questions of myself and what wound do I need to heal?

What impact did my father have on me?

What impact am I having on my sons?

What do I need to do differently?

What does God want to teach me about myself?

Have I missed the purpose of my calling at Eagle Brook Church? Is it more about I was called to fix me rather than to be called to fix the church?

As I think about who I am and what I do, I think I have lost some of my ability to ask the deep questions of the soul. I have focused more on asking questions about what someone does and less on who that person is. For some reason, I have moved away from asking the personal questions, even though I am in a role at a church where this should be desired and encouraged. This is one of the reasons why people view me as not caring or forgiving. I am not helping people find and fill their soul and am more focused on leadership and helping them do their job.

When I think of the relationship I had with my dad, I must say it was never a close one. I would never go to him with problems or seek his counsel. I never felt that I was accepted or good enough. He attended my activities but was not involved. I was pushed to be independent and do it on my own and by myself. I was driven to make my own success. In many ways, I was driven to accomplish things in my own power and I lived as though I did not need God. God blessed me with my intelligence and hard work ethic and with that, I thought I could do it on my own.

Besides my wife, Beth, who was the love of my life, I never had a close friend with whom I could open up and share my inner loneliness. I had friends that I would invest in, but the relationships were mostly about their needs and having fun. I am not sure I ever shared or was asked about my inner secrets or struggles. This re-enforced that I could do it on my own.

I had a great marriage, great jobs, financial success and I did not need God or anyone else to help me. I thought I was happy and fulfilled, but there was a void there that needed to be found and filled. I realized I was a fan of Jesus, but I was not a true follower of Him. My soul was empty because I was filling it up with success, family and work, but not with the peace that I needed. I was truly lonely, exhausted and running on empty. I just did not know it.

I had been rescued by the ending of my job at Target – being thrown out of the boat. It forced me to begin the process of letting go of control over my life and trying to trust God and give up control.

What is the wound in my soul that I needed to fix? It stems from never having a father figure in my life to care for me and be there when I was hurt and needing someone to support me. I pushed all of the hurt into drive and ambition. I called it a fear of failure, but I think the bottom line is it is more about being alone and never feeling like I truly had someone who loves me for who I am. I transferred the need in my soul to be loved to an attempt to fill that need with success.

Before coming on staff at Eagle Brook Church, I had people in my life who I was close to and who I was able to invest in and love. I also believed they returned that love. I could ask deep questions and discuss their lives, but I never truly discovered or shared the void that was in my own life.

When I had difficulties in my job after starting at Eagle Brook Church, the people who I thought were closest to me reinforced the behaviors I learned from my dad when I was young – you are on your own.

In reality, God was beginning to work on my heart. I was beginning to learn that what God wanted from me was my love and I learned that I needed Him. I looked for success, career growth, and adding value as a replacement for needing God. I could do it on my own. The arrogance that people thought about me was because I thought God had called me to improve Eagle Brook Church and that He gave me all the answers.

In reality, God called me to Eagle Brook Church to fix me and to learn that God is my Father. That He loves me and that He wants to be in this adventure with me. He wants to be by my side living it with me. I want others in my life, but they cannot be a replacement for having God as my Father.

I am so thankful for a dear friend who came on staff shortly after me who has been able to process through these learnings the past three years and be a person who showed he really cared about me and helped me learn about myself and how to change my perspective and thoughts. I am learning that coaching and leadership development is not about helping people to perform better in their jobs. It is about helping them discover who they are in God and allow God to be glorified through their actions. I need to come along side people and ask the questions about who they are and where is their soul's health and less about the task.

~~~

These learnings and exploration of my inner self, helped me understand why I had chemistry issues with people. My need and desire to be cared for by those closest to me actually often pushed me further away from them and caused relational conflicts. My abrasiveness often came because I failed to soften my soul first. This knowledge, I believe, actually helped me to be a better leader because I was able to focus on caring for them first and be less focused on the tasks that needed to be done.
~~~

Unfortunately, I had done a lot of damage along the way and it was hard for people who knew me from my early days to see or believe that I was really a different person. Those who got to work with me after making some changes experienced a very different me, and for that I was thankful.

I discovered my need for change in my character, and my need for change in my chemistry, and the third thing that I needed to remake was my **love for others**. I was raised in a home that focused more on the rules and less on the grace. My parents were a reflection of how they were raised and the rules and norms of their upbringing.

This philosophy was called fundamentalism and it created a house that was more focused on judging others for their sins than loving them so that God could change them. It was more about following a set of rules for behavior than looking at the heart.

Having this as my model, I was raised to be much more focused on Truth than on Grace. Not that the truth that I was taught and learned was wrong, but it left me as being the judge rather than allowing God to be judge. As I grew older, I learned how to tolerate people who were different than me, but not how to really love them as a child of God.

As I opened more of my heart to God, He started to soften my heart to love more. He taught me how to accept people who were not like me. He brought people into my life that became my friends who were different and came from different backgrounds, lifestyles or religious upbringing. He taught me that our job is to help people find and connect with God and to leave it to Him to convict and change their heart.

Finally, I learned that a relationship with God is not a set of rules to follow but rather learning to fill your soul with Him. What does that look like? **Being filled with God is manifested by the fruits of the spirit – love, joy, peace, patience, kindness, goodness, faithfulness, gentleness and self-control.** (Galatians 5:22-23).

Have I mastered all of these? No, but I am far better today than I was in 2012, five years ago. I will always be a work in progress until the day comes when I will be called to heaven to be with God forever.

REFLECTION QUESTIONS

- What has God been teaching you about what improvements or changes you need to make in your life?

- What are you reading to help you learn about God and his love for you?

- Who is in your life that knows that state of your soul?

- Who are you investing in to help them share their inner personhood?

10 | WHY SHOULD WE CARE

Then the Lord said, "You feel sorry about the plant, though you did nothing to put it there. It came quickly and died quickly. But Nineveh has more than 120,000 people living in spiritual darkness, not to mention all the animals. Shouldn't I feel sorry for such a great city?" Jonah 4:10 - 11 NLT

And that is how the book of Jonah ends. With a question from God – **"Shouldn't I feel sorry for such a great city?"** Most books end with a statement or what happens next to the main character, but not the book of Jonah. We don't hear from Jonah again. We don't know how he responded to God's question. Did he stay amongst the people of Nineveh and continue to teach about God? Did he go back to Israel and tell the people what happened? Until we get to Heaven, we will never really know.

What does this question at the end of Jonah mean for me? Do I feel sorry for the lost people around me? Am I willing to do whatever it takes to reach the people with the saving grace through Jesus? I think this is the question that influenced my decision to not go back to the corporate world and instead look for employment in ministry.

Most of my life I have been a Christian, but sadly, I cannot say my heart has broken for lost people. I would have been more on the truth side and less on the grace and love side of the equation. I looked at life through the lens that people were lost because of their own choices and it was up to them to change their behaviors, attend a church and find God. Of course, the attitude I had was not something that would be very appealing to those who needed God in the first place.

There was the feeling that you should change first and then you can be welcome. **How wrong I was!** The church is the place where people should be welcomed as they are and be loved so that they can understand God's grace and then allow God to transform their heart. **Perhaps, many people are not interested in a relationship with God because His followers are terrible at showing that they want a relationship with them!**

So back to this final verse in Jonah. This verse and the number 120,000 has stuck with me over the past five years. I feel that for whatever reason, God has called me to help reach 120,000 people. That is a daunting number and something that is truly God-sized.

Eagle Brook Church averages over 22,000 in attendance every week across six campuses. Being part of this great church was certainly part of reaching 120,000 people in the Twin Cities. With additional campuses being added in the future in addition to adding on-line services, I believe Eagle Brook Church will one-day reach over 120,000 people across the world.

But it is more than that. The goal of reaching 120,000 people is so God-sized that God wants me to be striving to accomplish this for the rest of my life. I used to think that I would retire one day, and then do what? I am learning that what God calls me to do will last a lifetime. I want to be striving to reach lost people until the day I hit the finish line and God calls me home.

I believe you and I must pour the wisdom and experience we have into those who will lead our churches, our businesses and our government in the future. If I can impact 10 people and they do the same, over several iterations of growth we will be exceeding 120,000 people impacted. Consider how many you can impact through the ten people God places in your life!

As we wrap up this chapter, think about how are you doing at reaching the lost people around you? Who could you be investing in to prepare them for their future? How can God use you in a powerful way? Instead of being like Jonah, a man who has not left much of a legacy, we can be a people who create lasting legacies by building into others and striving to share God's love with those who we can influence.

REFLECTION QUESTIONS

- What God-sized dream do you have?

- What will fuel you until the day God calls you home?

11 | OOPS IT HAPPENED AGAIN!

This is where the title of the book comes together! After five years at Eagle Brook Church, I felt thrown overboard again when my employment ended on February 28, 2017. I was once again unemployed and caught in a storm. It was sudden and unexpected, but having been there before, I knew that God was preparing me for His next calling.

As I shared previously, my time at Eagle Brook Church was really about God fixing me to become the man He wanted me to become. I learned a lot about myself and I believe that I have become a very different person and leader than I was when I started five years ago. God was preparing me for my next assignment. I thought that was for bigger roles within EBC, but God had other plans.

In the fall of 2016, my boss left Eagle Brook to take a position at another church. This opened up the job that I felt God had been preparing me for, to be the Executive Pastor. I thought I had the experience and background to be that person, and I felt God had prepared me to assume those responsibilities.

However, **that was not God's plan.** My peer was selected for the role and promoted into the position that I had hoped would be mine. This began a season of asking the questions of what is next for me? Is it to be content in the role that I had and serve my new leader or was God giving me a sign that He had something else for me.

I asked God for clarity regarding whether I should stay at Eagle Brook Church or resign to do something else and laid out a fleece to seek God's direction. My fleece this time was specifically around being allowed to write and share my thoughts in a personal blog. I posted one blog and I was told by leadership that I was not allowed to blog any more. God once again answered the fleece I placed before him. The answer was that it was time to leave Eagle Brook, but I chose to ignore it.

I worked hard at trying to find contentment in where I was. I had people that I wanted to continue to work with and help develop. We had campuses to open and more people to reach to get to the 120,000 that God had laid on my heart. Even though I knew in my heart my time to go was here, I pushed it off. I once again told myself that if I could just work six more years I could retire and then I would do what God wanted me to do.

You would think that I would have learned from my experience with Target, that when God gives you a clear message, you need to follow His direction. I guess I am a slow learner! God had plans for me, so once again I was thrown out of a job and into the sea.

On February 28th, 2017 I was called into the Senior Pastor's office and told that I was being let go. I was no longer a good fit and my employment was over. The reasons given tied back to comments I had made back when I was told that I would not be getting the Executive Pastor position in September 2016 and how I responded to the decision not allowing me to write a personal blog.

I may have forgotten the lesson about listening to God's calling, but I did remember what I learned after I lost my job at Target. While I still experienced pain and sadness at the unexpected job loss, I also knew that God was in control and this would not have happened if it was not part of His plan for my life. I also remembered how God had showed me through my fleece that it was time to leave.

I stopped trying to figure what I was going to do next, and instead just laid it before God. I asked God to show my wife and me what He wanted us to do next and to allow us to take the steps of faith to follow Him.

I wrote the following in my blog:

~~~

Have you ever experienced a week that has been full of surprises and emotional swings? Have you ever felt like you were where God wanted you only to find out that God has other plans for you?

It has been that kind of week for me! Last week my position
~~~

at Eagle Brook Church came to an end. It was a surprise and not what I was expecting, but it was a reality! This past week has been a week filled with emotional swings – it's as if I was on a roller coaster! I was dealing with feelings of loss, rejection, disappointment and questions of why, but I was also feeling a sense of excitement, relief, freedom and optimism.

This past week Beth and I have started each day with a prayer asking God to show himself to us in unexpected and powerful ways and at the end of the day we have talked about what we experienced that day and how God showed up. It has been truly an amazing time of experiencing God's presence and closeness in our lives!

On Monday, we went to see "The Shack." What a powerful presentation of what God's love is like! No matter what you feel about the theology of the movie, we walked out of the showing with tears running down our faces as we felt through the movie that this is how God has been showering His love on us this past week. God wants us to let go of our hurts, anger, disappointment and free us to be loved by Him and to love others. As shown in the movie, Jesus wants us to get out of our boats and walk on water with Him!

I don't know what my future holds or what I will be doing professionally tomorrow, next week or next month, but I know that God loves me and that He has a plan for my life. He wants a relationship with me and wants me to live fully in that relationship. I am going to take this new-found freedom to search for what God wants me to do with my life. I am going to spend a couple of weeks in Ukraine with our friends there and then I am going to spend some time writing a book that has been on my mind for several years and begin to blog my journey. I want to spend some time listening to God and allow Him to direct me in how I spend my time and energy professionally for the next season of my life.

Is it a little scary? You bet! But this is where God wants all of us. He wants us to let go of control and TRUST Him. His plans are better than mine and they are exactly what is right for me. This is hard to do for me as I am a control freak who likes to have everything figured out, but there is something very freeing and liberating to let go and shoot for the stars!

~~~

God works in amazing ways, that we often ignore or just say it is a coincidence. Back in December, before losing my job, my wife Beth was asked by a friend to speak at a women's conference in Ukraine. Beth asked me if I would go with her. I looked at my calendar, saw that it was open, asked for permission from my boss. He told me to go ahead and I booked our trip for March 16 – 31st of 2017.

After we purchased our non-refundable tickets, I realized that I had a conflict – this trip would be at the same time as the opening of Eagle Brook Church's new Anoka campus. This was something that I was supposed to be at, but would now have to miss. Little did I know that I would lose my job at the end of February and the trip to Ukraine would be exactly what we needed to heal and hear God's plans for our lives.

God knew when we booked our tickets in December that this was going to happen and I believe he blocked the dates of the grand opening for Anoka from my calendar and mind so that I would book the trip to be where He wanted us to be.

We went to Ukraine and God showed up in a big way. Some dear friends picked us up at the airport and we spent the day talking. Our friends could see a plan for me. A plan that I was not yet ready to see or expect, but it began the journey. We had numerous meetings over the next 10 days and God kept speaking to Beth and me. We were beginning to see the plan He was laying out for our future.

After Ukraine, Beth and I had several days together in our favorite place in Germany. It is a quaint spa town named Baden Baden. We had time to pray, talk and process what God was leading us to do. We talked about our passions and what God has been laying on our hearts. On our plane ride home, we read two different books. Beth
~~~

read "Divine Direction"[1] by Craig Groeschel and I read "Destiny"[2] by TD Jakes. Different books, but both brought clarity to what our next steps should be.

When we put our thoughts on paper, we realized we shared five common passions:

- Helping pastors.
- Helping churches.
- Investing in young leaders.
- Strengthening marriages.
- Helping the people in Ukraine.

These passions led us to start a non-profit company that will focus on helping Christian leaders to reach their full potential. We feel led to provide coaching, mentoring, training and strategic planning to pastors, church leaders, churches or other non-profits that need help.

God laid it on our hearts that He has richly blessed both Beth and I with tremendous experience and training over our years of employment in corporate jobs and within the church. One of the passages from the Bible that challenges me often is the following:

> *"When someone has been given much, much will be required in return; and when someone has been entrusted with much, even more will be required." Luke 12:48 NLT*

1 (Groeschel 2017)
2 (Jakes 2015)

This passage makes me ask the following question: **Am I doing enough with what God has given me?**

We have been given much over our years of working and ministry, so we feel that God is challenging us to use our gifts to help others. We decided we would create a non-profit organization that would allow us to do just that.

As we formed our non-profit, we wanted to create a mission that was focused on giving away what God has given to us and not ask people to pay for our services. We found it difficult to calculate what we needed to continue in ministry and only go when those financial needs were met. We would rather offer what we have to help anyone who asks for it, and to trust God will provide for the financial needs that we may have.

This next season of our life is a step of faith. We have felt God's direction and guidance each step of the way and we are committed to take one day at a time. We want to live by the following principle: What can we do today to help someone. Throughout this new season of venturing into the unknown, God has over and over said to us **"TRUST ME!"** And that is what we are going to do!

As I am writing this book, we have filed our paperwork with the IRS to gain 501(c)3 approval. This will allow us to receive tax deductible donations in the future. Our company's name is Potential Endeavors and our mission is **"Helping People Reach their Full Potential".** We have a board of directors and a business plan, but we do not have any clients and we do not know what we will be doing or who we will be doing it with. However, we know that we are on the path that God wants us to be on.

Over and over again as one door closes, God opens a new door and we meet new people with new needs and opportunities. What we are striving to do is find and follow the path that God has laid out for us.

Here are some of the verses from the Bible that we have found helpful on this part of our journey:

> *"Seek his will in all you do, and he will show you which path to take."* Proverbs 3:6 NLT

> *"Show me the right path, O Lord; point out the road for me to follow."* Psalms 25:4 NLT

> *"Make me walk along the path of your commands, for that is where my happiness is found."* Psalms 119:35 NLT

> *"This is what the Lord says: "Stop at the crossroads and look around. Ask for the old, godly way, and walk in it. Travel its path, and you will find rest for your souls."* Jeremiah 6:16 NLT

Just as the book of Jonah ended with a question, I want to end this book with a question for you. **What is the path that God wants you to take? Where do you need to take a step of faith today?**

BIBLIOGRAPHY

Eldredge, John. Wild at Heart: Discovering the Secret of a Man's Soul. Nashville, TN: Thomas Nelson, 2006.

Furtick, Steven. (Un)qualified: how God uses broken people to do big things. Colorado Springs, CO: Multnomah Books, 2016.

—. Crash the Chatterbox: Hearing God's Voice Above All Others. Colorado Springs, CO: Multnomah Books, 2015.

—. Sun stand still: what happens when you dare to ask God for the impossible. Colorado Springs, CO: Multnomah Books, 2010.

—. Sun stand still: what happens when you dare to ask God for the impossible. Colorado Springs, CO: Multnomah Books, 2010.

Groeschel, Craig. DIVINE DIRECTION: 7 decisions that will change your life. Grand Rapids, MI: Zondervan, 2017.

Idelman, Kyle. The end of me: where real life in the upside-down ways of Jesus begins. Colorado Springs, CO: David C Cook, 2015.

Jakes, T.D. Destiny: Step into Your Purpose. New York, NY: Hatchette Book Group, 2015.

Ortberg, John. Soul keeping: caring for the most important part of you. Grand Rapids, MI: Zondervan, 2014.

Rath, Tom; Conchie, Barry. Strengths Based Leadership: Great Leaders, Team and Why People Follow. New York, NY: Gallup Press, 2009.

Young, Sarah. Jesus calling: a 365-day journaling devotional. Nashville, TN: Thomas Nelson, 2008.

NOTES